Contents

Foreword

This publication, the second in our series and following on from Excellence in assessment and verification, *is aimed at people involved in the initial assessment of all learners. Initial assessment is critical to the success of the learning programme, as it provides a clear starting point for the learner and forms the basis for their progression to their desired outcome. Effective initial assessment will also improve retention and achievement on learning programmes. The guide gives an authoritative view of good initial assessment practice, and provides practical advice on how to ensure that your initial assessment meets the expectations of your learners.*

The guide follows our familiar style, in that it is produced to support the standards but focuses on developing your competencies to enable you to undertake effective initial assessment with your learners. It will show you how to ensure that learners are on programmes appropriate to them, how to assess their previous experience, and how to identify their preferred learning style and any barriers they might have in relation to achieving their desired outcome.

This guide has been co-authored by Hilary Read, a respected practitioner in the field of work-based learning, and Jane Wells, an occupational psychologist, a former lead inspector, now an associate, with the Adult Learning Inspectorate and an experienced initial assessment practitioner. In addition to the authors we have also benefited from the expert critique given by both practitioners and occupational psychologists.

I trust that this publication will support you as practitioners in providing high-quality initial assessment that benefits everyone involved in the learning cycle. Most importantly, it will enable you to make sure that the individual needs of learners are considered during the IA process, and that its results are used effectively and accurately to inform their learning plan.

David Morgan
Director, ENTO

Introduction

This guide is for you if you want to find out more about initial assessment and what it involves. It will enable you to see where initial assessment fits within the cycle of learning and development, and how it informs individuals' learning programmes and subsequent performance. Putting together an effective system of initial assessment can seem more complicated and time-consuming than it actually is; this guide will take you through the process step by step.

This section tells you who the guide is for, and how to use it, and explains the five key principles that form the basis of good practice in initial assessment.

Who the guide is for

This guide has been written for:

- trainers with responsibility for initial assessment

- people involved in recruiting learners to training and learning programmes

- trainers responsible for designing or planning learning programmes with learners

- those working towards achieving the Certificate in Support and Initial Assessment of Learning (and anyone else wishing to gain an overall understanding of the award)

- managers wanting to improve retention and achievement

- union learning representatives.

The benefits of effective initial assessment

The benefits of having a good initial assessment system are that learners will be better able to reach their own decisions about their learning programmes. It will help them make sure that they have chosen the right programme, and show them – and you – what they already know and can do and what they still need to learn.

Based on the five key principles described on pages 6–7, initial assessment should become an integral part of the induction process and inform your planning of each learner's individual learning programme. Accurate IA leads to tighter planning and targeting of learning provision, both of which result in improved retention and achievement rates.

Good initial assessment (IA) and effective learning plans are essential elements of all learning programmes, including:

- work-based learning

- apprenticeships

- learning programmes for getting people back into work or training

- rehabilitation programmes

- vocationally based higher education provision

- on-job training and development for employees.

The structure of the guide

The guide contains the following sections:

Introduction
This explains the key principles that underpin the guide and how to get the most out of it.

1 Getting started
This section tells you where initial assessment fits within the learning and development cycle, and shows you how to identify your values and write an effective IA policy.

2 Designing initial assessment
This explains the components that go into an initial assessment system.

3 Choosing and using initial assessment methods
This describes the different methods, the advantages and disadvantages of each and when to use them.

4 Using initial assessment to plan learning
This tells you how to use the results of initial assessment to plan and negotiate an individual learning programme (ILP) with learners.

5 Keeping it legal
This explains the impact of legislation on initial assessment and designing learning programmes.

6 Quality assurance (QA)
This shows you how to evaluate the effectiveness of initial assessment and explains how this forms part of your overall QA procedures.

7 Further information
This section lists some of the tools available.

Please note that where the guide refers to NVQs, this includes SVQs.

Key principles

Five key principles form the basis of good
practice in initial assessment, as follows:

1 All those with
responsibility for initial
assessment know exactly
what its purpose is and how
to carry it out effectively.

2 Initial assessment
focuses on the learner and
their needs, and includes
the learner in the process.

3 The results of IA are
used actively to inform the
ILP planning process.

This means:

- having policies and procedures
  in place and communicating
  these to staff

- training staff to use a range
  of IA methods and how to
  use the information gained
  from the process to plan
  learning programmes

- making sure that staff explain
  to learners the purpose of AI
  and what it involves.

This means:

- tailoring the IA process to meet
  individual needs and circumstances

- having a variety of methods at
  your disposal and using them
  with each learner over a period
  of time (effective IA is not
  something that can happen
  within a two-hour slot)

- taking account of the
  learner's opinions, needs
  and preferences.

This means:

- communicating the results of
  IA to those involved in the
  planning process

- feeding back the results of IA
  to learners

- knowing what options are
  available and how to communicate
  these clearly to learners

- working with learners so that
  they really do agree with the
  plan and are keen to follow it.

4 The initial assessment process is open, honest and transparent.

5 You identify all learners' learning and support needs in relation to the type and length of their programme, and ensure that these needs are met.

This means:

- all parties, including learners, are clear about the purpose of IA and what it involves

- having an IA policy that promotes equal opportunities

- making appropriate arrangements to ensure that all those who need to can access the results of IA, while complying with the Data Protection Act 1998

- using methods that are fair and open to scrutiny

- meeting the legal requirements

- evaluating your IA procedures regularly and acting on the results.

This means:

- building relationships with learners

- taking account of factors that affect learning.

1 Getting started

Putting together a detailed, integrated initial assessment system is well worth the effort: a growing body of evidence shows that organisations taking a comprehensive approach to IA have higher rates of retention and achievement than those that don't.

This section describes the ideal initial assessment system and the best way to approach the establishment of your own system.

Here are the steps you will need to take:

- *Identify your aims, values and the purposes of initial assessment, and write a policy explaining your approach and procedures*

- *Design your initial assessment system by constructing a flow chart and documenting your key procedures*

- *Train staff to achieve the Level 3 Certificate in Initial Assessment and Support of Learners*

- *Pilot and evaluate your system*

- *Make adjustments and implement them*

- *Feed the results of your evaluation into your QA system, monitor improvements and take further action if necessary.*

Where does initial assessment fit?

Put simply, a good initial assessment system tells you where the learner is at the start of any learning and development programme and gives an indication of where their learning needs lie. IA systems can fail when providers don't know what they are looking for, or are not good at putting together an individual learning programme for each learner.

Here's how initial assessment can inform learning and assessment at key stages of the learner's programme:

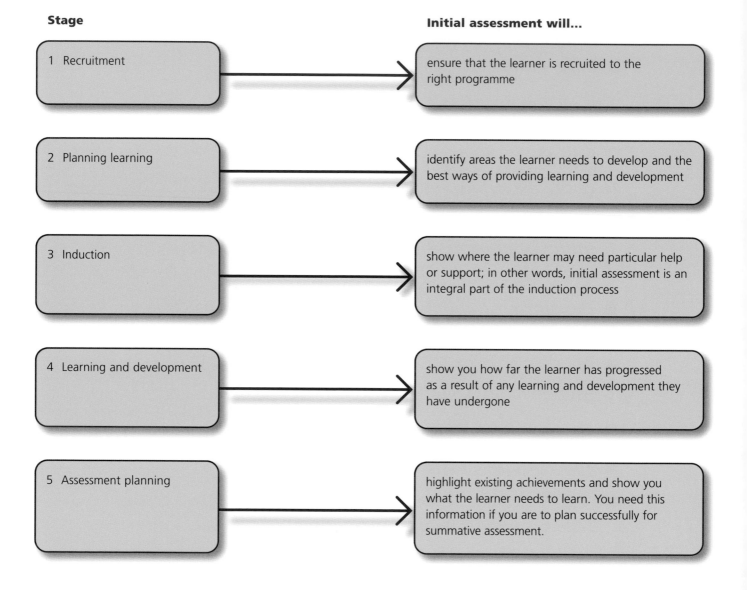

Stage

Initial assessment will...

1 Recruitment → ensure that the learner is recruited to the right programme

2 Planning learning → identify areas the learner needs to develop and the best ways of providing learning and development

3 Induction → show where the learner may need particular help or support; in other words, initial assessment is an integral part of the induction process

4 Learning and development → show you how far the learner has progressed as a result of any learning and development they have undergone

5 Assessment planning → highlight existing achievements and show you what the learner needs to learn. You need this information if you are to plan successfully for summative assessment.

Self-check

Use the following check questions to pinpoint areas where you need to do more work on your present IA policy and procedures. You are aiming to answer yes in each case. Where you answer no, turn to the relevant section of the guide for more help.

Question	Yes	No	Turn to...
Do we have formal procedures for initial assessment?	☐	☐	Section 2
Do we have a written policy?	☐	☐	Section 2
Do all who need to, know about our IA policy and procedures?			
• learners	☐	☐	
• staff	☐	☐	
• parents (where appropriate)	☐	☐	
• employers	☐	☐	
• schools/careers advice staff	☐	☐	
• others	☐	☐	Section 2
Do we know how to use each of the following methods of initial assessment fairly?			
• application forms	☐	☐	
• interviews	☐	☐	
• psychometric tests	☐	☐	
• in-house designed tests	☐	☐	
• self-assessment questionnaires and checklists	☐	☐	
• observation of group activities	☐	☐	
• assessment or evidence of previous learning, experience or achievement	☐	☐	
• work experience and work tasters	☐	☐	Section 3
Do we use the results of IA to plan learning?	☐	☐	Section 4
Does our IA system comply with current legislation?	☐	☐	Section 5
Is our IA system covered by our organisation's QA procedures? (Do we continually introduce and monitor improvements?)	☐	☐	Section 6

Towards an IA policy

It is a good idea to have a written policy and procedures for IA so that new members of staff, learners, parents or potential employers can understand what you are trying to achieve and what's involved.

Here are some of the elements or headings worth including in an IA policy:

Aims

- what you are aiming to achieve as a result of IA

Key procedures

- a flow chart documenting your key procedures

Individual learning plans (ILPs)

- your approach to ILPs (how the areas you initially assess link to the ILP, for example)

Methods

- a brief description of the methods you use (or intend to use), including:
  - how they are to be used and over what period of time
  - who will use them

Use of the results

- what you do with the results of IA in relation to:
  - planning ILPs
  - providing learning and development (the options available to learners and how you can provide them)
  - recording, storing and communicating the results

IA and the law

- how your procedures comply with current legislation

Other information

- the name of the person responsible for initial assessment and individual learning plans
- an annual review date
- the QA procedures you intend to use to evaluate the effectiveness of your IA policy and procedures, including people, resources, timescales and review dates.

Aims and values

A good place to start is to ask yourself: 'What are our values? or 'What are we promoting with our learners?' By identifying your core values (what matters to you most as an organisation), you will have identified the starting point for your initial assessment policy, as the following examples show.

Examples of aims and values

Here are some examples of aims and values set by training providers:

'We put the learner at the centre of everything we do.'

'Our company's mission is to identify every learner's strengths and to build on them.'

'We respect individuality and the differing needs of learners.'

'To encourage all trainees to achieve their maximum potential.'

'Our organisation values honesty and openness.'

'We aim to be at the heart of the community.'

'To maintain learners' dignity.'

'We are champions of equal opportunity in all areas of learning.'

'We value all learners' strengths and encourage their capability to learn and develop.'

'To identify and respond to what individuals can already do at the start of their programmes and to provide them with what they need to do to achieve their goals and targets.'

The last example provides a good aim for any initial assessment system.

Writing your own policy

Here are some pointers to help you when writing your initial assessment policy.

- Document your procedures using a flowchart. This is a visual and quick way for staff to gain a picture of the whole process. The example on page 15 will help you do this.

- Click on www.lsda.org.uk for further information on LSDA's publication *Improving initial assessment in work-based learning*, which explains how flow-charting can be used to improve initial assessment.

- Keep your policy brief: two or three sides of A4 at most.

- Include any examples of initial assessment instruments (tests, self-assessment checks, etc.) as appendices to your main policy. Try to include everything you use as part of the IA process.

- Write it as if you were explaining your approach and procedures to a new member of staff.

- Use short sentences and plain language. Explain any jargon or acronyms in footnotes or brackets as you go (your aim is for everyone to understand the policy).

- Get someone else to read through it and comment on whether it is easy to understand and whether or not you have included everything. Change it or add to it as a result of what they say.

One organisation's initial assessment policy

Initial assessment at ABC Training

1 Policy statement

We aim to accurately identify each learner's goals and aspirations and guide them to the appropriate course and programme. We will refer learners to other providers if we are unable to meet their needs.

2 Aim

The purpose of our initial assessment is to gather sufficient information to enable us to design a learning plan that reflects the learner's specific needs, and ensure that they have the best opportunity to attain their goals. We aim to ensure that each learner has a positive experience and achieves their potential.

2.1 Learning plan

When identifying what a learner needs to enable them to learn and achieve we will consider:

2.1.1 Their career aspirations and their relevant abilities and skills

2.1.2 The most appropriate learning programme for them

2.1.3 What they have already learnt and know, whether they have proof or not

3 Administration and standards

3.1 Initial assessment process

The initial assessment process will be comprehensive and gather information about:

3.1.1 Career aspirations/interests

3.1.2 Qualifications and achievements

3.1.3 Aptitude and potential

3.1.4 Prior learning and experience

3.1.5 Basic skill and/or key skill learning needs

3.1.6 Learning difficulties

3.1.7 Learning styles

3.1.8 Personal circumstances which may impact upon learning and achievement

3.2 Data Protection Act 1998

We will ensure that all our initial assessment activities comply with the relevant legislation with regard to data protection, by gaining learners' signed permission to collect and share information with appropriate others and keeping records in secure files accessed by named individuals only.

3.3 Equality of opportunity legislation

We will ensure that all our activities comply with the relevant legislation with regard to equality of opportunity, which is:

- Sex Discrimination Act 1975
- Race Relations Act 1976
- Race Relations (Amendment) Act 2000
- The Disability Discrimination Act 1995, as amended by the Special Educational Needs and Disability Act 2001
- Human Rights Act 1998

3.4 Our approach to initial assessment

We will ensure that:

3.4.1 Learners are fully involved in the initial assessment process

3.4.2 Learners understand the benefits of what they are being asked to do and how the information will be used

3.4.3 Learners agree how recommendations on learning requirements will be met

3.4.4 Feedback is given in a positive and encouraging way

3.4.5 Learners' views are collected during the initial assessment process

3.4.6 Initial assessment methods are appropriate

3.4.7 Assessment methods are monitored to ensure that they are effective and do not discriminate against certain groups of learners

3.4.8 Outcomes of initial assessment are recorded on an individual summary and used when designing the learning plan

4 Staff skills and experience

4.1 Training

All staff carrying out initial assessment will be appropriately trained. All staff will have attended XYZ's interview skills course and will be working towards the Certificate in Initial Assessment and Support of Learners.

Person responsible	Date of policy	Review date
Jo Smith	16 April 2004	16 April 2005

Example flowchart

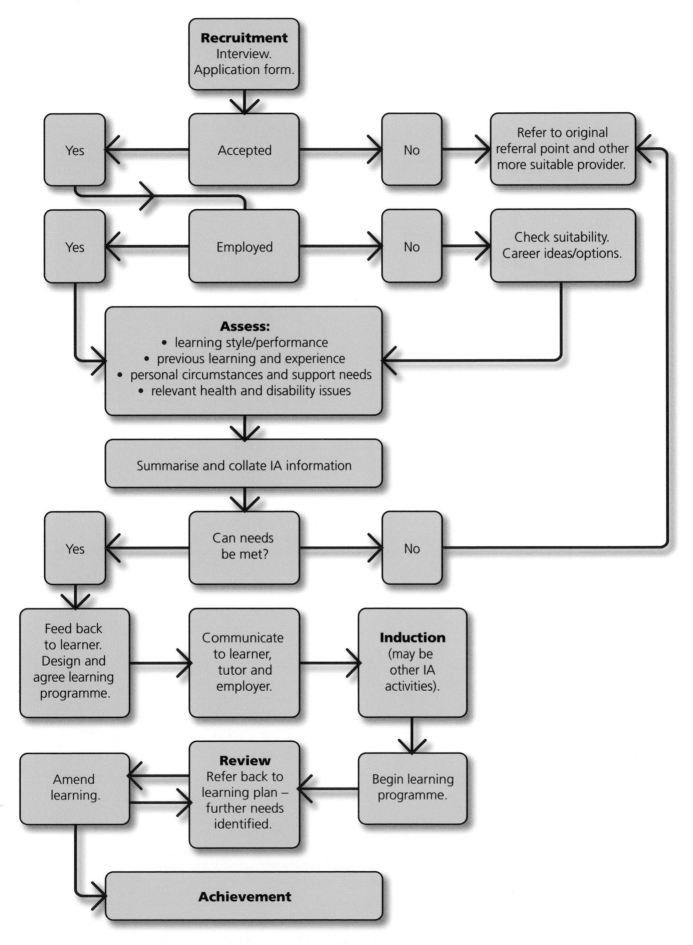

Recruitment
Interview.
Application form.

Accepted

Yes

No

Refer to original referral point and other more suitable provider.

Employed

Yes

No

Check suitability. Career ideas/options.

Assess:
- learning style/performance
- previous learning and experience
- personal circumstances and support needs
- relevant health and disability issues

Summarise and collate IA information

Can needs be met?

Yes

No

Feed back to learner. Design and agree learning programme.

Communicate to learner, tutor and employer.

Induction (may be other IA activities).

Amend learning.

Review
Refer back to learning plan – further needs identified.

Begin learning programme.

Achievement

2 Designing initial assessment

Overall, you are aiming to plan initial assessment so that it is useful and enjoyable from the learner's point of view, and encourages and motivates them to learn. If your learners are going to enjoy the IA process, you will need to include a variety of interesting activities and be prepared to spread them over a period of time. Most people enjoy finding out more about themselves and their abilities and preferences; they like answering questionnaires and appreciate getting feedback on their responses. The way you design your initial assessment system will also depend on the particular context and needs of your learners and any other people or organisations involved.

This section explains the main components of an initial assessment system.

It is important that perceptions and expectations are realistic. Learners' reasons for choosing a particular occupation aren't always the right ones. They can sometimes base their career decisions on unreliable sources of information such as TV programmes. ('The Bill' influences prospective police recruits and 'Casualty' and 'ER' influence prospective nurses.) Added to this, they may lack direct experience of their chosen career, or their peers, parents or teachers may unduly influence their decisions. As a consequence, many have unrealistic career expectations.

You can assess expectations effectively through constructing quizzes or by using more formal assessment methods.

Using online assessment

One university in south-east England had found that some applicants to nursing training had inaccurate ideas about what they would be doing on a day-to-day basis or what they would be studying. The university now uses an online assessment called New2Nursing, in order to gauge the expectations of their prospective nurses.

After they complete the assessment, applicants are given individual scores, along with accurate career information. This approach has significantly reduced the early leaver rate.

The main initial assessment methods used to assess occupational suitability are:

- career guidance tests or assessments

- work tasters or structured work experience

- discussion of hobbies, interests and career ideas.

Career guidance tests or assessments

Many career guidance tests and assessments are available. Traditionally, they ask respondents to choose between work characteristics that are then linked to particular careers or occupations. The theory underpinning this type of assessment has been influential since the early 1970s, when John Holland identified that people in similar jobs often have similar skills and interests (J. L. Holland, *Making Vocational Choices: a Theory of Careers*, Englewood Cliffs, NJ; Prentice Hall, 1973). These similarities can be grouped around:

- data – such as facts and figures

- ideas – such as thinking about new ways of doing things

- people – such as jobs with a social focus

- things – such as working with machines and equipment.

The following table shows some of the strengths and weaknesses associated with these tests and assessments. You need to weigh them up before deciding whether or not to add them to your initial assessment system.

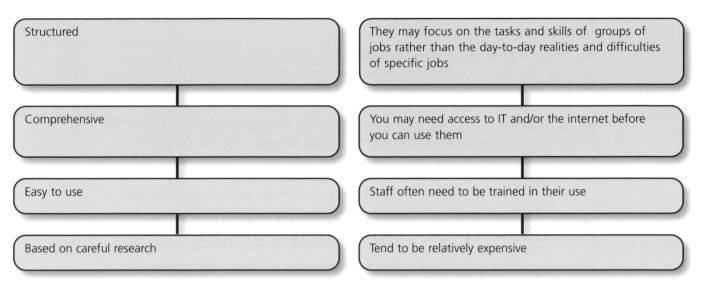

Strengths	Weaknesses
Structured	They may focus on the tasks and skills of groups of jobs rather than the day-to-day realities and difficulties of specific jobs
Comprehensive	You may need access to IT and/or the internet before you can use them
Easy to use	Staff often need to be trained in their use
Based on careful research	Tend to be relatively expensive

Work tasters

Work tasters are real-life, structured experiences set up within the workplace to provide a context for assessing someone's suitability for working in a particular occupation.

Here are the strengths and weaknesses of work tasters:

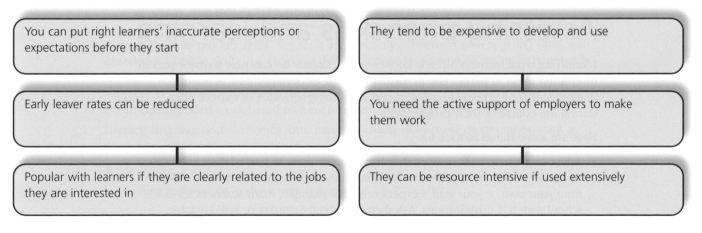

Strengths	Weaknesses
You can put right learners' inaccurate perceptions or expectations before they start	They tend to be expensive to develop and use
Early leaver rates can be reduced	You need the active support of employers to make them work
Popular with learners if they are clearly related to the jobs they are interested in	They can be resource intensive if used extensively

See section 3 for more information on choosing and using work tasters.

There is some overlap between key and basic skills. The new National Certificates in Adult Literacy and Adult Numeracy at Levels 1 and 2 are the same as the key skills tests in communication and application of number. Learners wanting to gain key skills qualifications need to produce a portfolio of evidence in addition to sitting the tests.

Here are some pointers for successful initial assessment of these skills.

- You are not trying to identify a deficit in the learner. Think instead in terms of building on what the learner already has, and use basic and key skills as a means of helping them achieve their learning goals.

- Talk positively about these skills. Say, 'You'll enjoy ICT; we bring laptops round to our learners and do the test on line', rather than 'Don't worry, we have special classes for people with reading difficulties.'

- Make sure you know the level of key or basic skills the learner needs in order to succeed in their learning programme, and that they have a realistic chance of achieving them. If you don't, you risk setting your learner up for failure before they start.

- Follow the key principles of including the learner in the process, using a variety of methods and assessing over a period of time.

- Ensure that you explain to learners what key or basic skills are and what you're looking for when you're assessing them initially.

- Be sensitive to your learner. Many people feel they have not been successful at learning key or basic skills, particularly if they have had negative experiences in the past. Putting them straight into a test situation probably isn't the best way of initially assessing them!

- Start with the wider key skills, particularly if your learners are beginning their programmes away from the workplace or don't have work experience (for example, school leavers or learners on E2E courses).

- Look for evidence of basic and key skills in the person's daily life. You might find examples of the skills applied to organising an outing, reading a timetable or writing a letter.

- If key or basic skills form part of a wider programme of learning (such as apprenticeships or NVQ learning), try and find ways of linking them to tasks or situations the learner can relate to in their place of work. In this way, you will help learners to see their relevance and minimise the fear factor.

- Avoid talking about basic and key skills in the abstract. They underpin day-to-day living and workplace tasks, so base any explanations around a situation that's meaningful to the learner.

Assessing learning support needs

Learners are all individuals with individual experiences and needs. As more people are encouraged to become learners, you will have to identify what additional support may be necessary in order to give each learner the best possible opportunity to achieve their chosen qualifications or targets.

Factors affecting learning

You need to find out what learning methods your learners have found helpful and enjoyed in the past, as well as the things that they found difficult. The best way of doing this is to ask them (though be sensitive about how you do this).

Here's how two different learners identified the factors affecting their learning.

A woman returning to part-time study

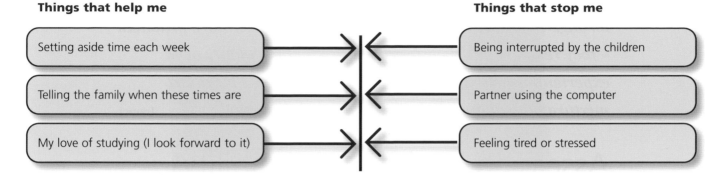

Things that help me   **Things that stop me**

Things that help me	Things that stop me
Setting aside time each week	Being interrupted by the children
Telling the family when these times are	Partner using the computer
My love of studying (I look forward to it)	Feeling tired or stressed

An apprentice in wood occupations

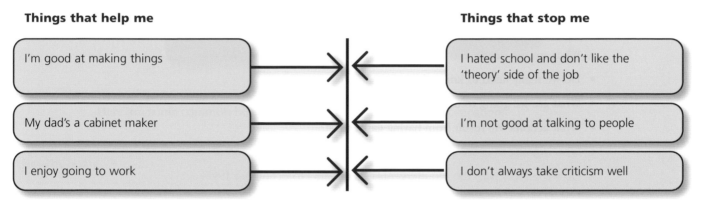

Things that help me	Things that stop me
I'm good at making things	I hated school and don't like the 'theory' side of the job
My dad's a cabinet maker	I'm not good at talking to people
I enjoy going to work	I don't always take criticism well

Examples like these can provide you with a good starting point for further discussion of support for the person's learning.

Learning preferences

Finding out how learners prefer to learn is helpful in managing their learning. However, research shows that there are many 'learning styles' models in use but that not all of them are based on valid or reliable information. (See *Learning Styles for Post-16 Learners: What do we know?* LSRC, 2004.)

You need to plan your approach when setting up your initial assessment procedures. Here are some overall considerations:

- Rather than using a one-off, 'learning preferences' model, think instead in terms of starting an ongoing discussion with each learner concerning the best ways of learning or approaching different tasks, then following this up as part of your review process.

- Avoid labelling learners according to their preferred learning style ('She's an activist – she likes learning by doing', or 'He likes reading and studying, he's a theorist.'). The best learners are those who can adapt their learning style to the circumstances. Encourage learners to try out new ways of doing things, even if it means making mistakes.

- Be clear about the purpose of assessing learning styles or preferences. Ask: 'Why are we doing this?' and 'What will we do with the results?' There's no point in raising learners' expectations concerning choice if you don't have the resources to back them up or don't intend to act on what they say.

- Use any information you gain about learners' preferred ways of doing things to help you improve the quality of teaching and learning within the organisation. Compare what actually happens with the ways in which learners say they prefer to learn, and identify areas where you could make changes or improvements.

3 Initial assessment methods

This section contains information about the main initial assessment methods, and will help you get the right balance between the subjective and objective ones.

The main methods to use are:

- *application forms*

- *interviews*

- *tests: psychometric tests and in-house tests*

- *self-assessment questionnaires and checklists*

- *observation of group activities*

- *assessing previous learning, experience or achievement*

- *work tasters.*

Subjectivity versus objectivity

Initial assessment can be carried out either objectively, subjectively or with a mixture of both. You need to use a range of different techniques to ensure that your IA is accurate and that learners get equal chances and opportunities.

You need to make sure that the whole IA process is flexible enough for you to be able to establish each learners' individual needs. At the same time, you should put checks and balances in place to ensure that you are being fair to everyone.

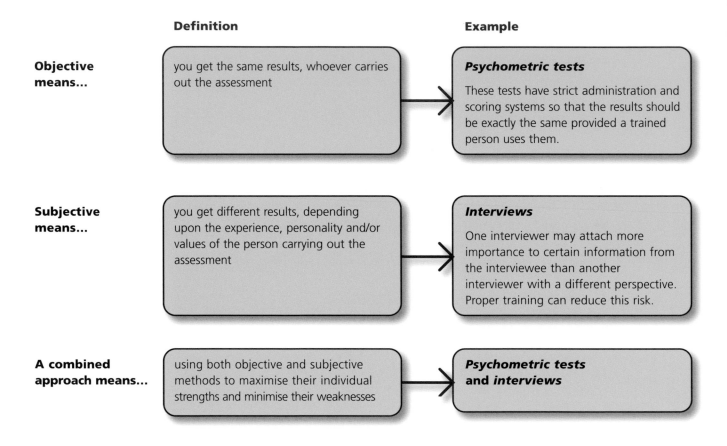

	Definition	**Example**
Objective means...	you get the same results, whoever carries out the assessment	***Psychometric tests*** These tests have strict administration and scoring systems so that the results should be exactly the same provided a trained person uses them.
Subjective means...	you get different results, depending upon the experience, personality and/or values of the person carrying out the assessment	***Interviews*** One interviewer may attach more importance to certain information from the interviewee than another interviewer with a different perspective. Proper training can reduce this risk.
A combined approach means...	using both objective and subjective methods to maximise their individual strengths and minimise their weaknesses	***Psychometric tests and interviews***

Application forms

Think of the application form as a starting point for other methods. Application forms are a good way of gaining basic, personal information about learners and specific information about any accredited learning and qualifications.

As with all the methods you choose, before you collect the information it is important to be clear about how you are going to use it. For example, if you wish to use your application form to identify basic or key skills levels, you must tell prospective learners that you intend to do this, so that they have a fair chance of showing you what they can do. (You would need to back this up with other methods to confirm attainment: application forms on their own are an unreliable indicator of attainment or potential.)

Strengths

The same information is requested in the same format from each learner

It's the most economical method of collecting personal information

Written applications can form the starting point for further exploration at interview

Weaknesses

Someone other than the learner may complete the form or contribute to completing the form

Some learners are better at expressing themselves in writing than others

Some learners may not pursue an application if they find form filling intimidating

Learners lacking self-confidence may not include information if they perceive it as irrelevant

What to include in an application form

Here's an example of an application form used with 16–19 year olds.

1 Personal

First name _____

Surname _____

Address _____

_____

Postcode _____

Telephone no _____

Date of birth _____

National Insurance no. _____

Nationality _____

Gender   Male ☐   Female ☐

> **Asking them to fill this in now saves time. You can always follow it up at interview or when you meet the learner.**

2 Education

Subject	Grade achieved	Grade I expect to get	Subject	Grade achieved	Grade I expect to get
English	____	____	Drama	____	____
Maths	____	____	Information technology	____	____
Science	____	____	Modern languages	____	____
Art/Design	____	____	Food technology	____	____
Business studies	____	____	Music	____	____
Geography	____	____	Other _____	____	____
History	____	____	Other _____	____	____

3 Are there any other achievements you would like us to know about?

(Include, for example, First Aid certificates, Driving Licence theory and/or practical, Duke of Edinburgh awards.)

> **You need to ask about other things. If you know your learners don't have many formal achievements, change the examples to things like: being a volunteer, organising or being a member of a group or club, looking after children or an elderly relative, etc.**

> **If they answer yes, you would want to follow this up during the interview, once you have established a relationship with your interviewee.**

4 Do you have a health issue or disability that may need additional arrangements or help, to enable you to work and/or attend a learning centre?

Yes ☐   No ☐

5 What is your ethnic group?

Asian or Asian British – Bangladeshi

Mixed white and Asian

Asian or Asian British – Indian

Mixed white and black African

Asian or Asian British – Pakistani

Mixed white and black Caribbean

Asian or Asian British; any other Asian

Any other mixed

Black or black British – African

White British

Black or black British – Caribbean

White Irish

Black or black British

Any other black

White any other

Chinese

Any other (write in) _____

Prefer not to say

> **You can explain that it's your policy to ask everyone this question**

6 How did you hear about us?

> **Include a question like this if you want feedback about your recruitment and/ or marketing methods.**

7 What are your reasons for wanting to join [the name of the learning programme]?

> **Treat this as a starting point for later discussion, rather than a way of assessing literacy levels.**

'We deliberately don't use a formal setting or we'd put our learners off. Many of them have had quite negative experiences of being formally assessed in the past, so we sit down with them in our coffee area and talk to them. However, we use the same interview format and ask the same questions of all our potential learners, so our procedure is fair.'   Training co-ordinator

Use the following checklist to help you when preparing for interviews. Aim to answer yes in every case. Space has been left for you to add any items you think are important.

Interview preparation checklist

Question	Yes	No
Is the furniture suitably arranged? (No head-to-head confrontations across a desk, or the interviewer's chair higher than the interviewee's, for example)	☐	☐
Is it a comfortable environment? (Warm or cool enough? Drinks available?)	☐	☐
Have I made sure we will be free from interruptions?	☐	☐
Have I made definite arrangements with the learner?	☐	☐
Does the learner know what to expect?	☐	☐
Do I know what I want from the interview and am I adequately prepared (with questions, tests, etc.)?	☐	☐
Other	☐	☐
Other	☐	☐

Non-verbal communication

We all communicate in different ways, and the words we use when we talk account for a very small part of our overall message. 'Body language', or more accurately non-verbal communication, can communicate up to 70 per cent of what we want to say or mean. Body language, just like any other language, varies between different cultures and societies. For example, in white British body language, engaging in eye contact is seen as positive, meaning that the person is paying attention and interested. However, in many other cultures making eye contact is a sign of disrespect or aggression. Trying to 'read' a learner's non-verbal communication is a specialist task, so unless you've been formally trained, don't rely on conclusions based on your understanding of body language.

There are four basic positions that you can look out for, however:

1 **open:** open arms and hands, both feet planted on the floor

2 **closed:** arms clasped around the body or folded so that hands do not show, legs crossed or wound around each other, legs turned away from the speaker

3 **forward:** leaning forward, shoulders slightly rounded, face looking forward

4 **back:** leaning back, playing with or attending to other things (fiddling with hair, or pieces of paper, etc.).

Let's look at what these positions can mean.

Learners in the closed position, with arms folded, legs crossed and bodies turned away, may be indicating that they are rejecting messages. Those showing open hands, facing you with both feet planted on the ground, are more likely to be accepting them.

Forward/back can indicate whether learners are actively or passively reacting to communication. When they are leaning forward and pointing towards you, they are more likely to be actively accepting or rejecting the message. When they are leaning back or their attention is elsewhere, they may be either passively absorbing or ignoring what is being said.

The combinations of open/closed and forward/back can give you clues about the learner's response:

- open/forward – the learner is likely to be responsive

- open/back – they are likely to be reflecting on what you are saying

- closed/back – they are likely to be feeling they want to escape

- closed/forward – they are likely to be actively resisting.

The easiest way to tell that a person is engaging in the interaction is that they are facing you with their body and feet pointing towards you and 'mirroring' your positions. If their head is facing you but their feet and body are pointing away from you, they may be feeling uncomfortable

Mirroring is when both people adopt the same position – as it would be if you were looking at each other in a mirror. Mirroring a learner's position is a good way to establish a rapport with them as it has a relaxing effect and indicates that you are both thinking similar thoughts.

Assessing motivation

One of the biggest problems encountered by trainers is that of learners' motivation. It's common to assume that all learners want to be on a particular programme at the beginning, when often the reverse is true. You can find out more about learners' motivation by exploring their reasons for wanting to join a particular programme with them. In doing so, you are aiming to help them find out:

- whether or not they want to be there (in some cases the parents or a line manager may be behind the decision to join)

- if they are ready to engage actively in learning.

If the answer is yes in both cases, the learner stands a good chance of succeeding. If, on the other hand, the learner answers no, you must face honestly the question of recruiting them or allowing them to continue. Dealing with learners' motivation at this stage will affect your future achievement and retention rates more than anything else. If you avoid the question, be prepared for potential problems such as dropping out or non-attendance at a later stage.

In-depth motivational interviewing involves using a set of principles to explore an individual's preparedness for change, and requires specialist skills. If you plan to explore learners' motivation, you need to have good counselling skills and some formal training in motivational interviewing.

Remember...

You will come across learners who appear very motivated at interview, and yet are some of the first to drop out. The reasons for this are that they may be good at interviews and come across well, or tell you what they think you want to hear, or they may just enjoy the challenge of the interview!

Reliability

When you use a test or assessment, you need to know that the results are as accurate as possible. No test or assessment will ever be 100 per cent accurate, as human beings are unlikely to behave in exactly the same way twice. The key, however, is to reduce the margin of error as much as possible to ensure that the test produces consistent results, as in the following example.

Perfect eggs every time

Imagine that you are trying to make the perfect scrambled egg. You follow the recipe exactly and use two eggs, a pinch of salt and a tablespoon of milk. You beat up the eggs with a fork, add the salt and milk and beat again. Next, you put a teaspoon of butter in the saucepan and use the middle-sized burner on your hob. You cook the egg for three minutes. On the first occasion you are really pleased with the results and decide to have scrambled egg again the next day. The next day the result is not as wonderful, even though you followed the recipe exactly as you did the day before. Your scrambled egg is almost the same, but not exactly.

When assessing the reliability of a test, you want to be sure that almost the same results but not necessarily 'exactly' the same results will be obtained whenever you use it. When you are sure about a test's reliability, this enables you to make comparisons between learners or to make judgements about the 'distance travelled'.

Validity

Validity is a technical assessment of the test's ability to measure whatever the test producer wants it to measure. So, if someone wanted to know how well you could drive a car, they would probably get into a car and go for a drive with you (they would be unlikely to ask you to accompany them on a bicycle ride!) There needs to be a good relationship between the topic of the test and what the test is being used for. It seems like common sense, but it can be very tempting to select parts of a test to save time, or use parts of different tests in the hope of producing a better test. Doing this will invalidate the test. In addition, commercial tests are usually protected by copyright legislation, so you would be breaking the law if you did this.

Standardisation in administration and interpretation

Psychometric tests are standardised. This means that there are prescribed ways of using the test, administering it, and interpreting the results. It is only by following the instructions on administration and interpretation precisely that you can be confident that the results are reliable.

Designing your own tests

Designing your own tests may seem like a cheap option, but it is most unlikely to give you the accurate results you need for good IA. Unless you have the technical expertise to design a sound test – a qualified occupational psychologist, for example – this approach is not recommended.

Self-assessment questionnaires

Self-assessment questionnaires and checklists are straightforward ways of gathering essential information for initial assessment purposes. They involve asking the learner direct questions about themselves or their performance. You can use them to:

- identify tasks that learners have done before or relevant experiences from their past
- gauge whether or not learners have access to particular opportunities (such as those necessary to gain a particular National Vocational Qualification)
- give learners the opportunity to assess their own strengths, weaknesses and support needs across a range of skills and abilities.

Self-assessments are straightforward to design. The key is to be clear about the areas where you want the learner to self-assess. Try to make it as easy as possible for the learner, by being specific and asking direct questions. For example:

Do you...	Yes – and I can prove it	I'm not sure	I need further help
know about your responsibilities under the HASAW Act?	☐	☐	☐
know about employers' responsibilities under the HASAW Act?	☐	☐	☐
know how to conduct a risk assessment?	☐	☐	☐
know about the different types of fire extinguisher and how to use them?	☐	☐	☐
keep an accident book?	☐	☐	☐
know what to do in the event of fire or an emergency?	☐	☐	☐

Strengths

- They are reasonably easy to construct and use
- You can gain a great deal of information relatively quickly
- Learners are actively engaged in assessing their own needs
- You can design them to be occupationally specific
- They are a good starting point for exploring further needs

Weaknesses

- Learners who are eager to present a positive self-image may overrate their abilities
- Research has shown that higher-ability learners' self-reports are more reliable than those of lower-ability learners
- Research has shown that females tend to under-report abilities while males tend to over-report abilities

Observation of group activities

Setting group tasks, then observing how learners perform, gives you the opportunity to look at a range of tasks from which inferences can be made about learners' abilities and learning support needs.

Observation lends itself to assessment of learners' ability to:

- communicate and work with others

- follow instructions

- work to deadlines

- solve problems.

'We used to sit them down and tell them about health and safety. Now we have three or four individual and group activities that they all do. We use this as a way of asking about how they prefer to learn and tackle things. They usually find it easier to work in a small group when answering the quiz questions, so we use this as a way of discussing team working.' Induction trainer

Getting it right

Observation requires careful planning and preparation, and you need to be aware of potential pitfalls. Here are some starting points.

- Observers need to be trained to observe as fairly as possible, otherwise you can be 'tricked' into being unfair. Some learners will attract your attention more than others, and you will be inclined to notice and judge them more frequently than you will others.

- One way to avoid 'over focus' is to construct behavioural statements rather than evaluative and subjective ones.

  For example, 'gets on well with others' means that the observer has to make a subjective, evaluative judgement about the behaviour of a learner. Two observers observing the same piece of action could come to different conclusions because they may disagree about what 'getting on well with others' means. An alternative – and fairer – statement would be 'spoke to group as a whole'. This is a statement that can be answered by 'yes' or 'no'. By watching a learner you can simply count how many times the learner spoke to the whole group.

Making the most of induction

It is worth looking at your induction process to see if you are making the most of existing group activities as opportunities for initial assessment. You may find ways of extending such activities or including new ones. For example, induction into an apprenticeship usually requires induction into equality of opportunity and health and safety. You can design these sessions to include observations of learners' skills and abilities, thus making the activity cost and time efficient.

Observing an equal opportunities session

The following example is taken from a session on equality of opportunity, where learners' abilities to discuss topics were being initially assessed.

For this sort of activity, you need one member of staff to run the session and another to run the observation. When observing more than two people, taking notes is not a reliable recording method. A better alternative is to use the 'five-bar gate' method. Here, you draw a line each time you observe someone demonstrating a particular behaviour, and then group the lines into fives, as shown on the chart below. This makes it quicker to interpret the results at the end of the exercise. This is not a pure science, but simply a way of structuring the means by which you make judgements about learners.

You will make fewer errors if you use a highlighter to colour each behavioural statement before you start, as you will quickly get to know the statement each colour represents. (This will be especially true if you regularly use the same rating grid.)

In this activity, a group of seven learners was asked to discuss five photos that they had been given. Their task was to decide what jobs each of the people in the photos did. They were given five job titles and had to allocate them to the photos. In the first part of the activity the group had to come to a decision that they all agreed with. The purpose of the activity was for learners to realise that you cannot make reliable judgements about people just by looking.

Communication skills	Sunita	Jo	Emma	Yeshim	Devon	Chris	James
Raised a new point	I	I	III		I		II
Spoke to the whole group	I	II	++++ III		I		IIII
Made relevant comments	II	I	I		II	II	IIII
Appeared to listen	I	III		I	I	I	II
Used positive body language	II	II		I	III	I	II
Summarised group discussion points	I				I		III
Made decision	I	I	++++		I		II
Spoke to one or two members of the group	I	I		IIII	I	II	I

Immediately you can see that Emma seemed unable to listen to other's contributions and dominated the activity, while Yeshim was very quiet and reluctant to speak to the whole group.

Learners can become angry if they feel they are not being judged fairly. Think about the following:

Unfair judgement

Two 15 year olds, Becky and Nicola, were doing work experience at the same company in the same office, but for different supervisors. One of the mothers of the two girls took them both to work each morning. At the end of the period each supervisor was asked to judge attendance as 'good', 'average' or 'poor'. Becky's timekeeping was judged as good, while Nicola's was judged as average. Both girls arrived at exactly the same time each day and, as a result, Nicola was very upset.

You can use observation of group activities in other areas, including:

- health and safety

- learning styles and preferences

- key skills (particularly the wider key skills of working with others and problem solving).

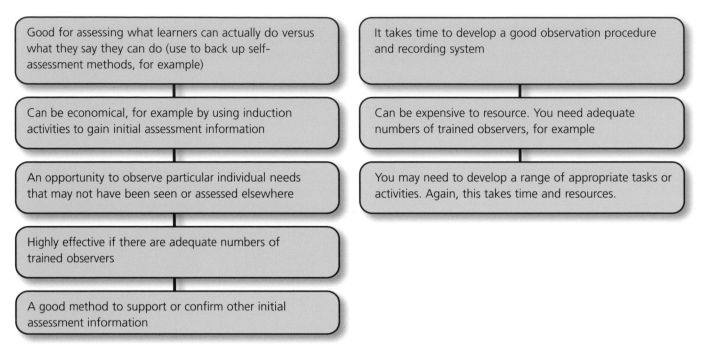

Strengths

Good for assessing what learners can actually do versus what they say they can do (use to back up self-assessment methods, for example)

Can be economical, for example by using induction activities to gain initial assessment information

An opportunity to observe particular individual needs that may not have been seen or assessed elsewhere

Highly effective if there are adequate numbers of trained observers

A good method to support or confirm other initial assessment information

Weaknesses

It takes time to develop a good observation procedure and recording system

Can be expensive to resource. You need adequate numbers of trained observers, for example

You may need to develop a range of appropriate tasks or activities. Again, this takes time and resources.

Evidence of previous learning

The best place to look for evidence of past learning or achievement is to ask learners for documentary evidence of what they have done. Exceptions to this would be those who have retired or who have been out of mainstream learning or employment for long periods. These learners may have little documentary evidence to show what they have done in the past. You need to handle this topic sensitively with them, focusing instead on discussions about other, positive day-to-day experiences of learning.

Documentary information

Several sources of documentary information may help you assess prior learning or achievements, and help you build up a picture of learners' attainments generally. These are:

- Progress File (or Record of Achievement)

- recruitment and appraisal information from employers

- curriculum vitae

- references

- qualifications

- records of training courses attended.

Documentary evidence	Useful for...	Weaknesses
Progress File	providing a comprehensive record of past experiences and achievements	Not all learners have one, or they may not see its usefulness.
Information from employers	preventing duplication of IA activities, provided you can rely on the quality of the information	Employers may be unwilling to allow access to specific information. You may not gain the 'whole' picture.
Curriculum vitae	giving you an overview of someone's career and learning	The individual chooses what goes in the CV (and what to leave out).
References	allowing you to check basic details such as the length of time someone has spent with a particular employer	Referees are often reluctant to put their true views in writing.
Qualifications	making judgements about what a learner knows or can do	There are huge numbers of qualifications: you need to know what they mean before you can make a reliable judgement.
Records of training courses	showing that the learner understands about learning	It can be difficult to know the content or quality of the course, and thus to make judgements based on them about what the learner knows or can do.

Work tasters

Using work tasters or work experience is a valuable way of ensuring that learners have a fair idea about what working in a particular industry will be like. If you decide to use work tasters as a method of initial assessment, you must first think about how to structure the experience so that you gain the information you need and can make fair or reliable decisions as a result.

Work tasters in dentistry

John Plummer Associates recruits and trains dental nurses. As part of the initial assessment and recruitment process, applicants spend one week in the dental surgery. Dental surgeons rate applicants using a set of behaviourally anchored rating scales. These are based on objective criteria, to ensure that there is consistency in the information gained and the judgements made, as different dental surgeons rate the applicants. The process helps the dental surgeons making the judgements to keep subjective opinions to a minimum.

Each prospective learner has a record on which individual grades are recorded. Judgements are made against a clear set of criteria, like this:

Presentation and appearance	Score				
Hair suitable for surgery hygiene	1	2	3	4	5
Uniform presentation	1	2	3	4	5
Jewellery conforming to surgery requirements	1	2	3	4	5

These criteria are supported by the following 'behaviourally anchored rating scales':

Hair suitability		Uniform presentation		Jewellery	
Hair clean, tidy and away from face	5	Clean and smart	5	No jewellery	5
Hair clean, needs minor adjustment, i.e. tied back	4	Clean and ready for work at the start of the day	4	Earrings of a sturdy nature	4
Hair clean and of appropriate appearance	3	Clean and presentable	3	Earrings or hair clips	3
Hair clean, untidy, needs constant adjustment	2	Not well presented	2	Any jewellery other than the above	2
Hair not clean or of an unprofessional style or colour	1	Not clean and tidy	1	Having been informed of health and safety, still wearing jewellery	1

All applicants are assessed in broadly the same way, reducing problems that occurred previously when dentists based judgements on whether or not they liked the applicant.

This method of structuring questions is also an effective way to ensure equality of opportunity. You could, however, argue correctly that some of the criteria in the above example are not strictly objective.

Here's an example of objective behaviourally anchored rating scales used to assess timekeeping:

Arrived for work before 8.50 am	4
Arrived for work between 8.50 am and 9 am	3
Arrived for work between 9 am and 9.10 am	2
Arrived for work after 9.10 am	1

Using self-assessment in work tasters

Another approach is to structure a self-assessment checklist for prospective learners to complete. This encourages learners to take an active part in assessing their own suitability, and encourages them to think more deeply about the implications of going into a particular industry. A useful extension of this technique is to ask prospective employers to complete the same checklist. When both have completed the list, prospective learner and prospective employer compare the similarities and differences. In this way any incorrect perceptions of the job and/or their abilities can be discussed.

Here are some examples of questions:

	Strongly disagree	Moderately disagree	Slightly disagree	Neither disagree nor agree	Slightly agree	Moderately agree	Strongly agree
I have a good attendance record							
I adapt well to new situations							
I treat health and safety very seriously							

Choosing the best method

The following chart shows you how you could use each assessment method.

	Interviews	Psycho-metric tests	Self-assessment questionnaires	Observation	Application forms	Evidence of previous learning, etc.	Work tasters
Basic skills	X	X	X			X	
Key skills	X	X	X	X			X
Wider key skills	X	X	X	X		X	X
Learning preferences	X	X	X	X			
Occupational suitability	X	X	X				X
Occupational and technical skills and abilities	X	X	X	X	X	X	X
Existing skills and knowledge	X	X	X	X	X	X	X
Personal skills	X	X	X	X			X
Learning support needs	X	X	X	X	X		X
Personal circumstances and other personal support needs	X		X		X		
Health or disability	X				X		

Initial assessment methods: test yourself

1 Which type of interview is likely to be the most effective when interviewing learners?

   a structured ☐

   b unstructured ☐

   c semi-structured ☐

2 Why can reading body language lead you to make incorrect assumptions?

   a body language is cultural ☐

   b some people have habits that don't reflect what they are really feeling ☐

   c sometimes we focus on one aspect of body language and don't seem to see the rest ☐

3 Psychometric tests should be well constructed so that they are reliable. What does this mean?

   a it gives exactly the right result 100% of the time ☐

   b it gives very similar results most of the time ☐

4 If you design your own assessments, in which you are going to score and make a judgement about an individual, what must you ensure?

   a they are reliable and valid ☐

   b they use questions that have been used in other psychometric questionnaires ☐

   c they look professional ☐

5 Self-assessment checklists can be problematic because:

   a learners lacking confidence may underrate their abilities and achievements ☐

   b learners can complete them quickly ☐

   c they are time-consuming to produce ☐

6 Why do work tasters help to reduce drop-out?

   a learners can have a taste of the reality of doing the job ☐

   b it gives employers the opportunity to reject the learner before they start properly ☐

   c learners can test out travel costs and times of public transport ☐

7 Look at the list of initial assessment methods. In each case, tick one column and say if you think it is objective, mostly objective, subjective or mostly subjective.

Method	Objective	Mostly objective	Mostly subjective	Subjective
Application forms	☐	☐	☐	☐
Interviews	☐	☐	☐	☐
Psychometric tests	☐	☐	☐	☐
In-house designed tests	☐	☐	☐	☐
Self-assessments	☐	☐	☐	☐
Observation	☐	☐	☐	☐
Evidence of previous learning	☐	☐	☐	☐
Work tasters	☐	☐	☐	☐

Test yourself: answers

1 Semi-structured

2 All statements are true

3 It gives very similar results

4 They are reliable and valid

5 Answer a is correct, answer b may also be correct if the person administering the checklist does not take sufficient care, and answer c is incorrect.

6 Answer a is correct, answer b may be technically correct but not to be encouraged, answer c may be correct but there is no research to support this.

7 Application forms......................Mostly subjective

Interviews ....Subjective or mostly subjective

Psychometric tests......................Objective

In-house designed tests

- if properly constructed ....Objective

- if not properly constructed ....Objective, but inaccurate and unfair

Self-assessments.........................Mostly objective

Observation...............................Mostly objective

Evidence of previous learning .....Mostly subjective

Work tasters ....Mostly subjective

4 Using initial assessment to plan learning

This section concentrates on what you do with the results of initial assessment. It gives detailed advice on how to plan and negotiate an effective individual learning programme (or plan) with each of your learners.

Individual learning plans (ILPs) are also known as:

- *personal development plans (PDPs)*

- *personal action plans (PAPs)*

- *individual training plans (ITPs).*

Whatever you decide to call them, learning plans can vary in style and scope. For short courses, they may be completed once and be very brief. For longer learning programmes, learning plans will be more complex and need to be regularly reviewed.

The key to effective planning is preparation. Once you have carried out initial assessment, you need to know how to use the information you have gained and turn it into a realistic plan for learning, with input and agreement from the learner.

Presenting options

Remembering verbal information can sometimes be a challenge, because being told something involves little active thinking on the listener's part. Similarly, if you give learners information to read in long paragraphs of small print on poorly photocopied white paper, they are unlikely to remember very much of it. They are more likely to remember information contained in short, punchy sentences presented as a series of bullet points.

You need to present learning and development options to learners in a variety of ways, for example:

- **verbally**: face to face or recorded orally for those with hearing impairment

- **written**: using simple language, or Braille for those with visual impairment

- **graphically**: using photographs, cartoons and diagrams in a visually stimulating manner (using different colours, shapes or sizes).

Using appropriate language

It is essential to communicate with learners using simple, jargon-free language, whether or not English is their first language. There are various ways of checking whether you are using language at an appropriate level, as follows:

- **SMOG (Simple Measure of Gobbledegook) testing** Analysing text using SMOG gives you a reading age. Click on www.basic-skills.co.uk, which contains a guide to making reading easier, including how to carry out a SMOG test on a piece of text.

- **Collins Cobuild dictionary** This gives a percentage according to how much a particular word is used. Words with a low percentage are less common and therefore best avoided. More information is available at: www.cobuild.collins.co.uk.

- using the **readability statistics** on the 'Tools' menu of your computer.

Getting learners to make decisions

Learners are far more likely to be committed to their individual learning plan if they make their own decisions about it. Giving learners feedback and realistic information helps them make informed decisions, but you also need to be able to put yourself in their place. Your learner may be feeling intimidated, powerless or alienated, or excited, eager and impatient. Their feelings can compromise their decision making, and they may simply go along with a plan because:

- they think you expect it

- they feel they don't have a choice

- they are desperate to change things in their lives and 'move on'

- they think it will please their parents or other people in positions of influence or power.

Getting learners to make decisions involves:

- developing a good rapport with them

- giving learners time to think or 'mull over' their options and consider the consequences

- listening carefully for hesitations and watching body language

- asking questions about their understanding.

Instead of repeating information, try asking questions instead (but avoid grilling them). Here are some ways in which you can ask instead of telling:

Instead of telling...	Try asking...
You will be coming into the centre on Wednesdays to do key skills.	Q. What will you be doing when you come into the centre? A. Key skills Q. What do you think 'key skills' are? Etc.
You will have a review with your assessor every 12 weeks.	Q. How often will you be having a review? Q. Who will do a review with you?
The review will involve looking at what you have done and setting targets for what you are going to do over the next three months.	Q. What do you think we'll be talking about during a review?

Remember...

The planning process means giving learners enough information to enable them to take part and make informed decisions.

You need to explain:

- *your equal opportunities policies and how these apply*

- *health and safety legislation and their responsibilities under the law*

- *the appeals procedure and how to use it*

- *confidentiality: what happens to the information about them and who sees it*

- *what's expected from them in terms of attendance at learning or training events*

- *the roles and responsibilities of all those involved in the learning process.*

What goes into the ILP

The results of initial assessment tell you about your learners' aspirations, attainments and potential as well as highlighting areas where they may need help. The purpose of the ILP is to turn this information into a realistic plan, with key targets based on each learner's particular needs and details of their route to achieving them.

The main things to include in the plan are:

- overall learning targets and, where appropriate, specific learning objectives

- learning activities (how the targets will be met)

- assessment and review

- who's involved

- resources needed

- dates and timescales for achievement.

Recording and communicating the ILP

The more you involve learners in physically writing and communicating their plans, the more they will be committed to them. You can do this by getting learners to:

- write down or key in their plan in the first instance

- customise or design their own plan

- go through it with their employers and tutors

- comment on their plan and update it as they progress.

Think in terms of helping the learner to think of the plan as theirs and to take ownership of it – this will increase their motivation. Be honest about what you can allow them to do. It's no good encouraging learners to make their own decisions if you don't have the resources or options available to support them.

It isn't enough to record an ILP and then file it away. All those involved need to see the plan. This means:

- briefing subcontractors, trainers and/or workplace supervisors concerning individual learners' needs, and involving learners themselves in this process

- meeting with employers and negotiating opportunities for learners to acquire and practise particular skills or tasks, or explaining what's involved in projects or assignments that the learner may be carrying out

- ensuring that the learner has a copy of their ILP and understands exactly what is happening, when and why.

'I ring them the day before they start their off-job training just to make sure they've remembered and that they've thought about how to get there.'

Trainer

'We negotiate learning projects with all our learners and employers. They see it as of benefit to their business.'

Placement officer

Planning learning: test yourself

Question	Possible answers	Tick one
1 Why is it important to give learners feedback on the results of initial assessment?	**a** So that they can make informed decisions	☐
	b So they can tell their parents or employer how well they are doing	☐
2 What is the most effective way to present options to learners?	**a** Verbally	☐
	b Written text	☐
	c Graphically	☐
	d A mixture of the above	☐
3 Why might learners sign a learning plan when they don't really agree to it?	**a** They just want to get started	☐
	b They feel they have no other option	☐
	c They want to please you	☐
4 How can learners participate in planning their learning?	**a** They can write it themselves	☐
	b They can update it themselves	☐
	c They can be responsible for communicating the plan to tutors	☐
5 Using simple language when communicating with learners is important because most learners have difficulties with literacy.	**a** True	☐
	b False	☐

Answers 1a; 2d; 3 & 4: all three are correct; 5b.

Learning targets and objectives

Use the SMART acronym to help you set effective targets that are:

- **S**pecific – defining clearly what is to be done
- **M**easurable – you are able to measure whether or not they have been achieved
- **A**chievable – they are realistic and the learner can achieve them
- **R**elevant – they are worth doing and relevant to the standards
- **T**ime bound – the target contains a time limit.

The best objectives are always 'SMARTER'. They are also:

- **E**njoyable and
- **R**ewarding.

Planning for assessment and review

Planning learning is not the same as planning for assessment, although you do have to include times when assessment will take place. You need to understand the difference between assessment planning and reviewing progress: these are two different processes. Use the review process to identify the point at which your learner starts to perform to the standards you intend to assess, otherwise you will waste time and learners will become demotivated.

'To be honest, until recently our planning process was driven by the assessment process. We need to focus more on learning and development – how the learner is actually going to learn the knowledge, skills and attitudes they need in the early stages of their programmes. We plan to introduce key skills learning right at the start of all our learners' programmes, as we know they underpin the vocational skills and actually help learners to acquire these once you've made the links.'

Training manager, hairdressing

How the ILP changes

As learners progress, so their ILPs change accordingly. At the **start** of the learner's programme you will be:

- setting overall targets and learning objectives to enable learners to acquire the necessary knowledge, skills and attitudes

- setting up appropriate learning activities, including catering for any special needs the learner may have

- arranging for assessment of prior achievements, if relevant.

In the **medium term**, learners need the opportunity to put into practice what they have learnt until they become confident and competent at what they are doing. At this stage, your job is to:

- modify existing learning objectives and add new, more challenging ones

- take appropriate action in areas where the learner is not making adequate progress

- find opportunities for the learner to put what they have learned into practice, particularly in the workplace

- recognise the point at which they are performing to standards (national or in-house), as this is when you should plan for summative assessment.

As learners near the **end** of their programmes you will:

- plan for summative assessment to take place

- arrange for certification

- take urgent action in areas where learners need remedial help with their learning and development.

Self-check

Once you have drawn up an ILP with a learner, you may find it helpful to ask yourself the following check questions. Aim to answer yes in each case. Where you answer no you will need to take action or alter the ILP accordingly.

Item	Question	Yes	No
The programme	Is the learner on the right one?	☐	☐
Qualifications	Are they achievable?	☐	☐
The overall targets	Are they based on the results of initial assessment?	☐	☐
	Are they realistic and achievable?	☐	☐
Learning objectives	Are they SMART objectives?	☐	☐
The activities	Are they suitable for this learner?	☐	☐
	Are they structured?	☐	☐
	Do they allow for learning to take place? (For example, does the learner have time to learn and apply what they have learnt before producing evidence for assessment?)	☐	☐
	If relevant, do they take account of opportunities for learning in the workplace?	☐	☐
	Are they relevant? (If I say yes, would my learners agree?)	☐	☐
Timescales	Are they realistic?	☐	☐
	Do they take account of particular circumstances such as seasonal changes in the workplace?	☐	☐
Involving the learner	Have I taken account of the learner's individual needs and preferences?	☐	☐
	Is the learner actively involved in their own learning? (Do I have proof of this other than a signature?)	☐	☐
Involving others	Does everyone involved know about the results of initial assessment?	☐	☐
	Does everyone involved know what's expected? (For example, have I communicated with college staff over the provision of any off-job training? Is the learner's employer supporting any work-based learning?)	☐	☐

5 Keeping it legal

You need to ensure that your initial assessment activities and learning plans comply with current legislation. This section will help you take stock and identify possible areas for action.

The two main areas of legislation that apply to initial assessment concern equality of opportunity and use of information.

Legislation concerning equality of opportunity

The Sex Discrimination Act 1975

The Race Relations Act 1976

The Race Relations (Amendment) Act 2000

The Disability Discrimination Act 1995 as amended by the Special Educational Needs and Disability Act 2001

The Human Rights Act 1998

Legislation concerning the use of information

The Data Protection Act 1998

Sex discrimination

The Sex Discrimination Act 1975 makes it unlawful to discriminate on grounds of sex in employment, education and advertising, or when providing services. There are three kinds of illegal sex discrimination:

- **direct** — because of someone's sex

- **indirect** — because conditions have been set that appear to apply to everybody, but really discriminate against one sex

- **victimisation** — when a person is discriminated against for taking action under the Act.

In planning and implementing your initial assessment process, you need to make sure that your initial assessment activities are fair to both genders. This means:

- asking the same or similar questions of both males and females

- not using tests or assessments that unfairly disadvantage one group

- checking that your entry requirements (or those of your employers or subcontractors) do not require skills, qualifications or knowledge that may disadvantage one gender over another. (For example, boys are more likely to have an ICT GCSE than girls.)

Entry requirements

Occupations with broadly equal gender balance such as retail and hospitality tend to be open in entry requirements and look for qualities such as enthusiasm and commitment. Female-dominated occupations also request similar attributes and emphasise good communications and interpersonal skills. In contrast, male-dominated occupations set tighter requirements such as precise numbers of GCSEs, subjects and grades.

QPID Study Report Series *Modern Apprenticeships and Gender Stereotyping*, March 1999.

Racial discrimination

The Race Relations Act 1976 prohibits direct or indirect racial discrimination on account of a person's race or ethnic origin. As with the sex discrimination legislation, you need to be aware of both direct and indirect discrimination:

- **direct** racial discrimination means treating someone less favourably because of his or her race, colour, ethnic origin or nationality

- **indirect** racial discrimination is the setting of conditions which, while seeming to apply to everyone, actually discriminate against certain people.

To ensure that you comply with the law you should:

- take account of cultural differences in body language in your initial assessment interviews (see section 3)

- ensure that any tests or assessments do not disadvantage one group over another because of the way they are designed, administered or scored

- review all tests, assessments, documents and interviews for culturally free language — for example, questions such as 'Do you enjoy working with people who have airy-fairy ideas?' could discriminate against those whose first language is not English.

The Race Relations (Amendment) Act 2000 strengthens and extends the scope of the 1976 Race Relations Act, and places a duty on the public sector actively to promote equality of opportunity.

Discrimination on disability grounds

The Disability Discrimination Act 1995 (as amended by the Special Educational Needs and Disability Act 2001) aims to end the discrimination that many disabled people face. The Act gives them rights in the areas of education, employment, access to goods, facilities and services and in the buying or renting of land or property. In education and training, this applies to admissions procedures as well as to access to leisure facilities and accommodation.

The Act describes disability as:

'a physical or mental impairment which has a substantial and long-term effect on a person's ability to carry out normal day-to-day activities. The disability is to have lasted or be likely to last 12 months or more. If a person has had a disability within this definition, they are protected from discrimination even if they are no longer disabled.'

The key principle of the Act is that you have a duty to be *anticipatory*. In initial assessment this means:

- you know how to make reasonable adjustments to the tests or assessments you currently use, so that they would be accessible by someone with a visual or hearing impairment, for instance

- you ensure that the learning plan is based upon a learner's individual needs rather than designed around what is available.

Things to think about...

Delivering separate sessions to a learner with a disability on the ground floor, while similar, group sessions are available elsewhere, means denying this learner the benefits of peer support and group interaction. Using timed tests can put some learners with disabilities at a disadvantage.

Human rights

Article 8 of the Human Rights Act 1998 concerns the right to respect for private and family life. It means that everyone has the right to respect for their private life, their family life, their home and their correspondence. Public authorities cannot interfere with this right, except:

'as is necessary in a democratic society [...] for the protection of health or morals, or for the protection of the rights and freedoms of others'.

When gathering information for initial assessment, you need to:

- be clear about your reasons for asking for personal or sensitive information

- make sure that if you ask for health information it is in order to protect the health of the individual or that of other trainees/employees.

The law is to do with balancing the rights of individuals against protecting the rights and freedoms of others. (Public authorities can justify their exemption to Article 8 in certain circumstances, whereas a private individual or company would not be able to override Article 8 in the same way. If you are not a public body, you may not be an exception under the law.)

Using information

The Data Protection Act 1998 regulates the processing of information relating to individuals, including the obtaining, holding, use or disclosure of such information. This applies to all personal information, held electronically or otherwise.

All the information you obtain as a result of initial assessment is covered by the Act, including

- individual learning plans
- information within the learning plan that is to be shared with third parties (for example, employers, assessors and verifiers)
- application forms
- interview records
- test and assessment results and decisions
- email communications containing personal information about specific learners.

To comply with the Act, take account of the following:

1 You and any others who decide how and why personal data are processed (the Act calls these 'data controllers') need to be open about how you use those data and to comply with data protection principles in your information-handling practices.

2 Your learners have the right to have a copy of all the information that your organisation holds about them.

3 Your learners have a right to object to you processing personal data concerning them.

4 You only keep information for as long as is strictly necessary.

5 You must seek learners' permission before you pass on any information to a third party. This includes employers, tutors and anyone else involved in the learning process.

6 Under the first principle of the code, learners have a right to see the information you hold on them, and by law you must tell them:
   - what the information you collect will be used for
   - who will process it
   - who it will be passed to.

Here is an example of how one organisation has met the requirements of the Act.

ABC Training
Data Protection Statement

So that your training programme can be designed for you as individually as possible, we need to collect some information about you. We may use a range of methods to do this and these are detailed below. When we have collected this information our staff, including the tutors, will have access to it. In addition, various statutory* bodies will be able to see it. These include the Learning and Skills Council, who will be contributing to the funding of your programme, and the Adult Learning Inspectorate, who may inspect the quality of the learning programme that you are receiving. In order to comply with the Data Protection Act 1998 we need your permission to share the information that you give us with appropriate bodies. Please sign against each of the items below to confirm that you agree to the information being seen.

Information source	Signed	Date
Interview records		
West Notts Keyskillbuilder		
Basic Skills Agency literacy assessment		
Basic Skills Agency numeracy assessment		
Observation notes of personal and social skills activities		
Individual Learning Plan		

You are entitled to see any of the personal information that we hold about you. Please ask us, at any time, to see your personal records. We may need seven days' notice to prepare this.

We will not pass any personal information to a third party unless we have your permission to do so.

Signed _____ Manager, ABC Training.   Date _____

* A statutory body is an organisation that has been established by statute (law) and has the full backing of Parliament.

Self-check

Use your answers to the following questions to help you identify areas where you may need to take action. Only tick yes if you can prove that it is happening in practice.

Area of compliance	Yes, and we can prove it	Not sure	No
Do our IA procedures and practices mean we operate within the law on			
• direct sex discrimination?	☐	☐	☐
• indirect sex discrimination?	☐	☐	☐
Do our IA procedures and practices mean we operate within the law on			
• direct racial discrimination?	☐	☐	☐
• indirect racial discrimination?	☐	☐	☐
Are we anticipatory with regard to the needs of learners with disabilities?	☐	☐	☐
Do we respect all learners' rights to privacy?	☐	☐	☐
Do learners know what information we hold about them and who sees it?	☐	☐	☐
Have we obtained learners' permission to hold and use this information?	☐	☐	☐

You are aiming to answer yes in all cases. Where you have ticked not sure or no, you must take action to ensure that you comply with legislation in these areas.

6 Quality assurance

Quality assurance (QA) of initial assessment and individual learning plans should form part of your organisation's overall quality assurance framework. It's important to monitor what you do over time and to have a formal plan concerning the areas you want to look at. The information you gain will tell you whether or not your IA procedures are working, and point you to further changes or improvements.

The QA cycle

The QA cycle looks like this:

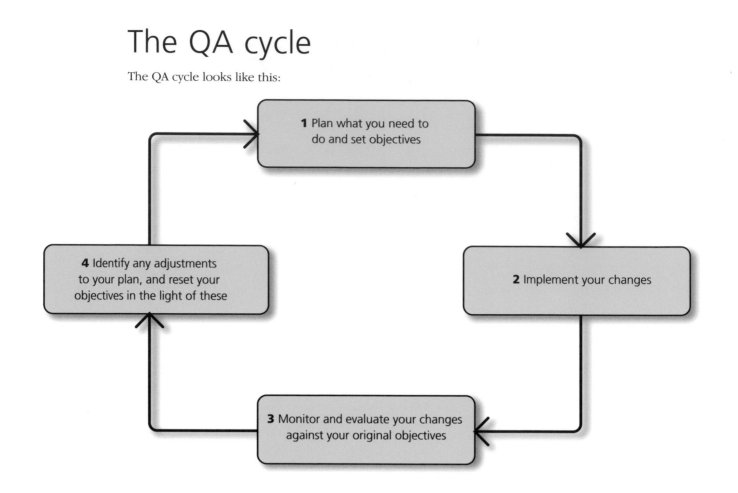

You keep going round the cycle as you plan, collect information and monitor, evaluate and reset your objectives as a result. In this way you will improve your initial assessment system continually over time.

'It was recommended that we include observation of IA with our internal verification procedures, so when our verifiers observe assessors in action we also look at our initial assessment procedures and how well these are working.'

Training provider

Quality assurance and initial assessment

Quality assurance of initial assessment and learning plans involves:

- observing staff carrying out key initial assessment and planning activities
- checking how initial assessment tests and assessments are used and interpreted
- gathering feedback from learners, employers and trainers
- sampling the quality of learning plans on a regular basis
- using your findings to make decisions about continuous improvements.

You may wish to look at the following four areas in more detail.

1 Observing what happens in practice

Initial assessment activities that lend themselves to observation include:

- interviews
- how initial assessment tests are administered
- feedback to learners
- negotiating learning plans with learners.

'When we sent each of our co-ordinators in to observe how tests were being administered in each of our centres, we realised our procedures were inconsistent – and unfair to learners overall. Some administrators were letting learners take as much time as they needed, while others were giving them a time limit.'

Training co-ordinator

2 Sampling

Sampling means looking in more depth at a representative selection of assessments or plans. You might consider sampling the scoring and interpretation of the tests or assessments you use and the quality of individual learning plans.

Here are some questions to set yourself:

- Are we scoring and interpreting the results of tests and assessments correctly, according to the instructions?
- Are the decisions we are making based upon the results of initial assessment? Are they consistent among different members of staff and/or different occupational areas?
- Are we recording the results of initial assessment consistently, and are all learners getting the same or broadly similar access to support from the outset?

3 Gathering feedback

This is where you actively seek feedback from learners, tutors, employers and any others involved in the process. Do this by using formal methods such as questionnaires or follow-up telephone interviews.

7 Further information

This section lists some of the tools available for use in your initial assessment practice, and describes relevant qualifications and training. It also explains the work ENTO does and the Learning Network it runs.

Initial assessment packages

Here are some of the products available that may be suitable for initial assessment. Before you investigate further, make sure that:

- you have a rough idea of what you are looking for

- you have audited your current practice and provision, and you can show how the package will meet an identified need

- buying in a package is the best way of meeting your own and your learners' initial assessment needs

- you can show how the package forms part of an overall, planned system of initial assessment.

(Please note that ENTO does not endorse the following products. These are a sample of what is available.)

Name	Type	Content	For more information, click on...
Fast Tomato	Online	Questionnaire Career, course and place suggestions Options at years 10 & 11 and after year 11 Local information Hints and tips	www.fasttomato.com
Kudos (15–18 year olds) and Adult Directions (for 19+)	CD	Careers matching Skills matching Careers database Personal view of jobs General information	www.cascaid.co.uk
CID	CD	Careers database Careers information on over 880 jobs Photographs and videos Links to the internet	www.careersoft.co.uk
Careers Advantage	CD	Combination of: • Pathfinder – helps learners match skills, interests and abilities with suitable careers • Odyssey – occupational database with more than 950 job titles	www.progressions.co.uk

Name	Type	Content	For more information, click on ...
FEATS (Future Education and Training Series)	Paper based	Assessment consisting of four modules: 1 Key word/number skills 2 Writing skills 3 Visual processing 4 Personal qualities Vocational guidance questionnaire Users need a BPS certificate in testing level A to administer and give feedback	www.nfer-nelson.co.uk
West Notts Basic and Keyskillsbuilder	CD	Fully interactive and self-marking Gives clear indication of current numeracy and literacy levels and predicts possible achievement Specified to national standards for basic and key skills Signposts subsequent diagnostic assessments to be taken Stand-alone PCs or networked	www.keyskillbuilder.ac.uk/
MAPs	Computerised or manual	A series of processes and products for assessing an individual's motivation and self-esteem	www.jca.biz/maps.htm

Training and qualifications

Level III in Advice and Guidance NVQ

The Advice and Guidance NVQ is aimed at those working directly with clients, giving out information or advice and offering them guidance.

The award comprises eight units: four mandatory and four optional.

Certificate of Occupational Testing (Level A and Level B)

This is awarded by the British Psychological Society. (See www.bps.org.uk for further details.) Level A is aimed at those involved in ability testing and level B at those doing personality testing. You will need this qualification for some products (such as FEATS), as only trained users can purchase them.

About ENTO

ENTO is an independent, self-financing organisation. Since 1988 its purpose has been to develop national vocational standards and qualifications (NVQs) and to provide products and services to support these standards and qualifications.

Our work helps people develop their level of competency and skills, and aims to meet the needs of learners, employees and employers as well as learners. We are also responsible for promoting and monitoring the matrix standard, a quality standard for any organisation that gives information, advice and guidance.

ENTO represents, across all sectors, those whose occupation requires them to deal with people in the workplace. This includes people in the field of information, advice and guidance; learning and development trainers; HR people; recruitment consultants; trade union representatives involved in learning; and health and safety at work practitioners.

Because of this role, people for whom ENTO standards and qualifications have been developed have a significant influence on the take-up of vocational qualifications throughout the workplace and at all levels. ENTO maintains 9 suites of National Occupational Standards covering 11 occupational areas, 23 NVQs, 4 Apprenticeships and 3 suites of non-qualification-based standards.

The Learning Network

The Learning Network is a membership-based professional development network run by ENTO for assessors and verifiers across all sectors and disciplines. The network's main aim is to enhance the continuous professional development of assessors and verifiers, by equipping them with up-to-date information, providing a forum for discussion and sharing of best practice, and the opportunity to influence what is happening in the arena of assessment and verification.

If you would like to join the Learning Network, or find out more, please email: info@ento.co.uk

Alternatively, you can click on: www.thelearningnetworkonline.com